MW01712847

THIS BOOK BELONGS TO:

Aderyn Publishing
Thunder Bay – Ontario – Canada

ISBN: 978-1-7778578-1-3

Aderyn Publishing
Thunder Bay, Ontario
Canada

aderynpublishing.com

Order information:

Quantity sales: Special discounts are available on bulk purchases by corporations, associations, organizations, and others. For details, contact the publisher.

email: admin@aderynpublishing.com

Welcome to this step in your tarot journey!

TABLE OF CONTENTS

Welcome i

How this book is set up iii

How to use this book v

SECTION ONE
Card Draws & Reflection Questions

Tarot Journey Reflection: Beginning Questions 3

Cards 1 to 30
- Card draws beginning with card 1
- Reflection questions for cards 1 to 30

Cards 31 to 60
- Card draws beginning with card 31
- Reflection questions for cards 31 to 60

Cards 61 to 90
- Card draws beginning with card 61
- Reflection questions for cards 61 to 90

Tarot Journey Reflection: Completion Questions

SECTION TWO
Resources & Tracking

List of cards drawn in order with trend tracking 131

List of cards drawn by date 135

My notes about each card 139

My list of questions 151

SECTION THREE

Journal & Notes pages 153

BONUS SECTION

3-Card Spread 163

Dear Tarot Reader,

The purpose of this book is to help you deepen your relationship with and understanding of your Tarot cards one card at a time using single card draws. If you are learning the Tarot, drawing one card at a time is a great way to become familiar with each card without the risk of getting overwhelmed by trying to learn and interpret multi-card spreads. If you are already familiar with the Tarot, this book offers the opportunity for you to go deeper with your cards by focusing on just one card at a time.

The various sections in the book are designed to help you interact with your cards in different ways. In your hands, you hold a notebook, workbook, trends tracker and journal all in one. And, over time as you work through the 90 cards and fine tune your understanding of them in the resources section, you will also be developing a tool that you can refer to again and again.

Every effort has been made to provide as much space as possible for writing, whether notes about the cards or journaling out thoughts, experiences or trends that are revealed to you as you go along and when you complete your journey.

Note: This book dœsn't aim to teach the Tarot. There are many different and excellent teachers to learn the Tarot from. Alternatively, you may want to just go within yourself and find your own meanings and interpretations. Or, mix it up and do both! Whichever way you choose to do it, use this book as your place to capture your growing knowledge, intuition and experience on this journey.

I wish you all the best as you go forth!

Sincerely,

Soaring Raven

How This Book Is Set Up

The book is made up of 3 main sections and 1 bonus section.

Section One - Card Draws & Reflection Questions

Section One has the pages for your single card draws. The pages are divided into 3 groups of 30 cards each: Cards 1-30, Cards 31-60, and Cards 61-90. As the cards are drawn randomly, it was thought that 90 draws would be enough to allow each card in your deck to show up at least once.

Card Draw Pages

On each of the card draw pages there is space to write your question, the context for your question if you want to include that, and the name of the card you pull. There is space to make notes about the card from your own thoughts and/or your teacher's interpretations, if you are working with or referring to a teacher. And there is space to write what message you take from the card in response to your question.

For added detail, there are places to put the date and time of day, the deck you are using, the moon phase, and the element the card is associated with if it is a Minor Arcana. Each page also has a box where you can either put your own illustration of the image on the card or describe it in words. There is also space to write keywords associated with the card. And to help, there is a reminder on each page for you to enter the card onto the tracking pages in Section Two.

Reflection Questions

Section One includes reflection questions before you begin your journey. Then there are reflection questions at the end of the 3-card spread section.

Page numbers in this section

Standard page numbers have not been used in Section One. Instead, the Card Draw pages are numbered sequentially from 1 through 90. This number is located at the top centre of the page. The Reflection Question pages are also unnumbered. Page numbers continue in Section Two.

Section Two - Resources & Tracking

This section contains 4 different subsections that can be filled in as you work through drawing your 90 cards. They are:

- **List of Cards Drawn in Order** (p. 131-134): These pages will give you an overview of all the cards you drew and the order you drew them in. There is also a place to note whether it was a Major or Minor Arcana card and which suit, if applicable. The related element of the card can also be noted here. This will reveal any trends in the types of cards you are drawing, if this is of interest.

- **List of Cards Drawn by Date** (p. 135-138): Even though you will pull 90 cards, you might not actually pull every card in the deck during this time! Only your Tarot deck knows which cards will be revealed to you! To that end, use these pages to mark the date or dates the cards were drawn on (if at all). At the end of the 90 days, you will be able to see which cards, if any, were drawn more than one time and which, if any, were not drawn at all.

- **My Notes About Each Card** (p. 139-149): These pages are where you can compile a master list of keywords for each card in the deck.

- **My List of Questions** (p. 151-152): These pages are for you to make note of questions that you could ask before picking a card. As you come across or create questions that you like and want to remember, put them in this section so you can refer to them.

Section Three - Notes

This section (p. 153-162) is for journaling and/or making any other notes you care to make.

Bonus Section

This bonus section (p. 163-171) has pages for 3-card spreads. Six of these pages have been added for you to use. A couple of additional lined pages for more notes or journaling can be found at the end of this final section.

How to use this book

Begin by looking through the different sections of the book to become familiar with its layout. Note that there are dark edges on the Section title pages to help with navigating the book.

When you are ready to begin your journey, start by working through the questions in the **Tarot Journey Reflection: Beginning Questions**. These begin on page 3 in Section One.

Once you complete the initial reflection section, start doing your single card draws and making your notes about the cards you draw.

Single Card Draw Session

Set yourself up in a comfortable location to prepare yourself and your Tarot deck. If you have a meditation routine or other steps that you do to prepare, do them. Then fill in the section at the top of the first card page with the date, etc. Next, formulate your question and write it down. If you want to include the context for your question, briefly write that down, too.

When you are ready, randomly draw one card. This card is Card 1. For the next time, your next random card will be Card 2, and so on through the 90 card draws.

Next, consider the card and make notes about it in the lines provided. These could be your interpretation of it or if you are learning from one of the many excellent Tarot teachers out there, you could include notes from their interpretations.

At the bottom of the page, make note of any keywords that you associate with the card. You can at any time turn to the page called **List of Cards Drawn in Order** in Section Two and enter the card name there, too, and indicate the element and type of card you pulled (ie. Major or Minor Arcana, etc). These pages begin on page 131. Here you will keep track of all of the cards you draw. This page will also show you if there are any trends or themes in the cards you are drawing.

Next, find your card on the **List of cards Drawn by Date** pages in Section Two and enter the date on the line beside the card name. These begin on page 135. Note: there is a reminder at the bottom on the right of every card draw page to enter the card on these tracking pages so you'll never forget.

After you have completed the first 30 draws, answer the reflection questions on the pages that immediately follow those card draw pages.

Then it's onto the next 30 draws again followed with reflection question pages. A third set of thirty pages will complete the 90 card draws.

Timing of Your Card Draws

There is no right or wrong time frame for how often you draw a card. Do what works best for you. Here are some ideas:

- pull a card every day for 90 days. (Note: this is the approximate number of days in a yearly quarter)
- pull a card everyday Monday to Friday
- pull 1 card in the morning and 1 in the evening
- go your own speed and pull a single card only on the days you want to

Finally, after drawing 90 cards, answer the questions that follow Card 90 in regards to the final 30 cards you drew. Then answer the questions in the **Tarot Journey Reflection: Completion Questions** to reflect on your full 90-card journey. Use the card lists to see if there were any trends that are interesting or notable for you.

Other Resource Pages

As you go along on your journey, and as you feel comfortable, write in keywords for the cards in the **My Notes About Each Card** (beginning on page 139) and compile your own list of questions on the **My List of Questions** pages (beginning on page 151).

When you are done your journey or at any time along the way, use Section Three for journaling or capturing any other notes, thoughts or ideas you may have about the Tarot and your experience.

If you wish to do some 3-card spreads, use the pages in the Bonus Section to do these and record your notes. They begin on page 163.

One final point: the cards mentioned in this book are from the Rider-Waite Tarot deck, but feel free to use any Tarot deck or decks that you would like.

Happy journeying!

SECTION ONE

Card Draws & Reflection Questions

Tarot Journey Reflection

- Beginning Questions -

What is my motivation or inspiration for studying the tarot?

How intuitive do I feel as I begin this journey?

How comfortable am I now with tarot cards as I begin this 90 card process?

What do I hope will happen from this study of the tarot?

My teachers and guides are:
(Or, am I working with only my own interpretations?)

What card deck or decks will I use? What are my thoughts and/or feelings about this deck?

Other thoughts and feelings I want to record at the start of my journey:

My Card Draws

for

Cards 1 to 30

Date:

Time:

Card:
1

Tarot Deck:

Moon Phase:

The Question I Am Asking Today:

The Card Drawn:

Related element:
◯ Fire ◯ Earth
◯ Water ◯ Air

Notes or interpretation for this card:

Describe in words or draw the card

In answer to my question, what message or guidance can I take from this card?

Keywords for this card:

I have entered this card on the:

◯ List of Cards Drawn in Order (pg 132)

◯ List of Cards Drawn by Date (pg 136, etc)

Date:

Time:

Card: 2

Tarot Deck:

Moon Phase:

The Question I Am Asking Today:

The Card Drawn:

Related element:
- Fire
- Earth
- Water
- Air

Notes or interpretation for this card:

Describe in words or draw the card

In answer to my question, what message or guidance can I take from this card?

Keywords for this card:

I have entered this card on the:
- List of Cards Drawn in Order (pg 132)
- List of Cards Drawn by Date (pg 136, etc)

Date:

Time:

Card:
3

Tarot Deck:

Moon Phase:

The Question I Am Asking Today:

The Card Drawn:

Related element:
- Fire
- Earth
- Water
- Air

Notes or interpretation for this card:

Describe in words or draw the card

In answer to my question, what message or guidance can I take from this card?

Keywords for this card:

I have entered this card on the:
- List of Cards Drawn in Order (pg 132)
- List of Cards Drawn by Date (pg 136, etc)

DATE:

TIME:

CARD:
4

TAROT DECK:

MOON PHASE:

THE QUESTION I AM ASKING TODAY:

THE CARD DRAWN:

RELATED ELEMENT:
◯ FIRE ◯ EARTH
◯ WATER ◯ AIR

NOTES OR INTERPRETATION FOR THIS CARD:

DESCRIBE IN WORDS OR DRAW THE CARD

IN ANSWER TO MY QUESTION, WHAT MESSAGE OR GUIDANCE CAN I TAKE FROM THIS CARD?

KEYWORDS FOR THIS CARD:

I HAVE ENTERED THIS CARD ON THE:

◯ List of Cards Drawn in Order (pg 132)

◯ List of Cards Drawn by Date (pg 136, etc)

Date:

Time:

Card: 5

Tarot Deck:

Moon Phase:

The Question I Am Asking Today:

The Card Drawn:

Related element:

- ◯ Fire
- ◯ Earth
- ◯ Water
- ◯ Air

Notes or interpretation for this card:

Describe in words or draw the card

In answer to my question, what message or guidance can I take from this card?

Keywords for this card:

I have entered this card on the:

- ◯ List of Cards Drawn in Order (pg 132)
- ◯ List of Cards Drawn by Date (pg 136, etc)

Date:

Time:

Card:
6

Tarot Deck:

Moon Phase:

The Question I Am Asking Today:

The Card Drawn:

Related element:

- ◯ Fire
- ◯ Earth
- ◯ Water
- ◯ Air

Notes or interpretation for this card:

Describe in words or draw the card

In answer to my question, what message or guidance can I take from this card?

Keywords for this card:

I have entered this card on the:

- ◯ List of Cards Drawn in Order (pg 132)
- ◯ List of Cards Drawn by Date (pg 136, etc)

Date:

Time:

Card: 7

Tarot Deck:

Moon Phase:

The Question I Am Asking Today:

The Card Drawn:

Related element:

- ◯ Fire
- ◯ Earth
- ◯ Water
- ◯ Air

Notes or interpretation for this card:

Describe in words or draw the card

In answer to my question, what message or guidance can I take from this card?

Keywords for this card:

I have entered this card on the:

- ◯ List of Cards Drawn in Order (pg 132)
- ◯ List of Cards Drawn by Date (pg 136, etc)

Date:

Time:

Card:
8

Tarot Deck:

Moon Phase:

The Question I Am Asking Today:

The Card Drawn:

Related element:
- ◯ Fire
- ◯ Earth
- ◯ Water
- ◯ Air

Notes or interpretation for this card:

Describe in words or draw the card

In answer to my question, what message or guidance can I take from this card?

Keywords for this card:

I have entered this card on the:
- ◯ List of Cards Drawn in Order (pg 132)
- ◯ List of Cards Drawn by Date (pg 136, etc)

Date:

Time:

Card: 9

Tarot Deck:

Moon Phase:

The Question I Am Asking Today:

The Card Drawn:

Related element:
- Fire
- Earth
- Water
- Air

Notes or interpretation for this card:

Describe in words or draw the card

In answer to my question, what message or guidance can I take from this card?

Keywords for this card:

I have entered this card on the:
- List of Cards Drawn in Order (pg 132)
- List of Cards Drawn by Date (pg 136, etc)

Date:

Time:

Card:
10

Tarot Deck:

Moon Phase:

The Question I Am Asking Today:

The Card Drawn:

Related element:

- ◯ Fire
- ◯ Earth
- ◯ Water
- ◯ Air

Notes or interpretation for this card:

Describe in words or draw the card

In answer to my question, what message or guidance can I take from this card?

Keywords for this card:

I have entered this card on the:

- ◯ List of Cards Drawn in Order (pg 132)
- ◯ List of Cards Drawn by Date (pg 136, etc)

Date:

Time:

Card:
11

Tarot Deck:

Moon Phase:

The Question I Am Asking Today:

The Card Drawn:

Related element:

- ◯ Fire
- ◯ Earth
- ◯ Water
- ◯ Air

Notes or interpretation for this card:

Describe in words or draw the card

In answer to my question, what message or guidance can I take from this card?

Keywords for this card:

I have entered this card on the:

- ◯ List of Cards Drawn in Order (pg 132)
- ◯ List of Cards Drawn by Date (pg 136, etc)

Date:

Time:

Card: 12

Tarot Deck:

Moon Phase:

The Question I Am Asking Today:

The Card Drawn:

Related element:

- ◯ Fire
- ◯ Earth
- ◯ Water
- ◯ Air

Notes or interpretation for this card:

Describe in words or draw the card

In answer to my question, what message or guidance can I take from this card?

Keywords for this card:

I have entered this card on the:

- ◯ List of Cards Drawn in Order (pg 132)
- ◯ List of Cards Drawn by Date (pg 136, etc)

DATE:

TIME:

CARD: 13

TAROT DECK:

MOON PHASE:

THE QUESTION I AM ASKING TODAY:

THE CARD DRAWN:

RELATED ELEMENT:

- ◯ FIRE
- ◯ EARTH
- ◯ WATER
- ◯ AIR

NOTES OR INTERPRETATION FOR THIS CARD:

DESCRIBE IN WORDS OR DRAW THE CARD

IN ANSWER TO MY QUESTION, WHAT MESSAGE OR GUIDANCE CAN I TAKE FROM THIS CARD?

KEYWORDS FOR THIS CARD:

I HAVE ENTERED THIS CARD ON THE:

- ◯ List of Cards Drawn in Order (pg 132)
- ◯ List of Cards Drawn by Date (pg 136, etc)

Date:

Time:

Card: 14

Tarot Deck:

Moon Phase:

The Question I Am Asking Today:

The Card Drawn:

Related element:

- ◯ Fire
- ◯ Earth
- ◯ Water
- ◯ Air

Notes or interpretation for this card:

Describe in words or draw the card

In answer to my question, what message or guidance can I take from this card?

Keywords for this card:

I have entered this card on the:

- ◯ List of Cards Drawn in Order (pg 132)
- ◯ List of Cards Drawn by Date (pg 136, etc)

Date:

Time:

Card:
15

Tarot Deck:

Moon Phase:

The Question I Am Asking Today:

The Card Drawn:

Related element:
- ◯ Fire
- ◯ Earth
- ◯ Water
- ◯ Air

Notes or interpretation for this card:

Describe in words or draw the card

In answer to my question, what message or guidance can I take from this card?

Keywords for this card:

I have entered this card on the:
- ◯ List of Cards Drawn in Order (pg 132)
- ◯ List of Cards Drawn by Date (pg 136, etc)

Date:

Time:

Card:
16

Tarot Deck:

Moon Phase:

The Question I Am Asking Today:

The Card Drawn:

Related element:

◯ Fire ◯ Earth
◯ Water ◯ Air

Notes or interpretation for this card:

Describe in words or draw the card

In answer to my question, what message or guidance can I take from this card?

Keywords for this card:

I have entered this card on the:

◯ List of Cards Drawn in Order (pg 132)

◯ List of Cards Drawn by Date (pg 136, etc)

Date:

Time:

Card:
17

Tarot Deck:

Moon Phase:

The Question I Am Asking Today:

The Card Drawn:

Related element:
- ◯ Fire
- ◯ Earth
- ◯ Water
- ◯ Air

Notes or interpretation for this card:

Describe in words or draw the card

In answer to my question, what message or guidance can I take from this card?

Keywords for this card:

I have entered this card on the:
- ◯ List of Cards Drawn in Order (pg 132)
- ◯ List of Cards Drawn by Date (pg 136, etc)

Date:

Time:

Card: 18

Tarot Deck:

Moon Phase:

The Question I Am Asking Today:

The Card Drawn:

Related element:

- Fire
- Earth
- Water
- Air

Notes or interpretation for this card:

Describe in words or draw the card

In answer to my question, what message or guidance can I take from this card?

Keywords for this card:

I have entered this card on the:

- List of Cards Drawn in Order (pg 132)
- List of Cards Drawn by Date (pg 136, etc)

Date:

Time:

Card:
19

Tarot Deck:

Moon Phase:

The Question I Am Asking Today:

The Card Drawn:

Related element:
- Fire
- Earth
- Water
- Air

Notes or interpretation for this card:

Describe in words or draw the card

In answer to my question, what message or guidance can I take from this card?

Keywords for this card:

I have entered this card on the:
- List of Cards Drawn in Order (pg 132)
- List of Cards Drawn by Date (pg 136, etc)

Date:

Time:

Card:
20

Tarot Deck:

Moon Phase:

The Question I Am Asking Today:

The Card Drawn:

Related element:

- Fire
- Earth
- Water
- Air

Notes or interpretation for this card:

Describe in words or draw the card

In answer to my question, what message or guidance can I take from this card?

Keywords for this card:

I have entered this card on the:

- List of Cards Drawn in Order (pg 132)
- List of Cards Drawn by Date (pg 136, etc)

Date:

Time:

Card:
21

Tarot Deck:

Moon Phase:

The Question I Am Asking Today:

The Card Drawn:

Related element:
- Fire
- Earth
- Water
- Air

Notes or interpretation for this card:

Describe in words or draw the card

In answer to my question, what message or guidance can I take from this card?

Keywords for this card:

I have entered this card on the:
- List of Cards Drawn in Order (pg 132)
- List of Cards Drawn by Date (pg 136, etc)

Date:

Time:

Card:
22

Tarot Deck:

Moon Phase:

The Question I Am Asking Today:

The Card Drawn:

Related element:

- Fire
- Earth
- Water
- Air

Notes or interpretation for this card:

Describe in words or draw the card

In answer to my question, what message or guidance can I take from this card?

Keywords for this card:

I have entered this card on the:

- List of Cards Drawn in Order (pg 132)
- List of Cards Drawn by Date (pg 136, etc)

Date:

Time:

Card:
23

Tarot Deck:

Moon Phase:

The Question I Am Asking Today:

The Card Drawn:

Related element:

◯ Fire ◯ Earth
◯ Water ◯ Air

Notes or interpretation for this card:

Describe in words or draw the card

In answer to my question, what message or guidance can I take from this card?

Keywords for this card:

I have entered this card on the:

◯ List of Cards Drawn in Order (pg 132)

◯ List of Cards Drawn by Date (pg 136, etc)

Date:

Time:

Card:
24

Tarot Deck:

Moon Phase:

The Question I Am Asking Today:

The Card Drawn:

Related element:

- Fire
- Earth
- Water
- Air

Notes or interpretation for this card:

Describe in words or draw the card

In answer to my question, what message or guidance can I take from this card?

Keywords for this card:

I have entered this card on the:

- List of Cards Drawn in Order (pg 132)
- List of Cards Drawn by Date (pg 136, etc)

Date:

Time:

Card:
25

Tarot Deck:

Moon Phase:

The Question I Am Asking Today:

The Card Drawn:

Related element:

- Fire
- Earth
- Water
- Air

Notes or interpretation for this card:

Describe in words or draw the card

In answer to my question, what message or guidance can I take from this card?

Keywords for this card:

I have entered this card on the:

- List of Cards Drawn in Order (pg 132)
- List of Cards Drawn by Date (pg 136, etc)

Date:

Time:

Card:
26

Tarot Deck:

Moon Phase:

The Question I Am Asking Today:

The Card Drawn:

Related element:

- Fire
- Earth
- Water
- Air

Notes or interpretation for this card:

Describe in words or draw the card

In answer to my question, what message or guidance can I take from this card?

Keywords for this card:

I have entered this card on the:

- List of Cards Drawn in Order (pg 132)
- List of Cards Drawn by Date (pg 136, etc)

Date:

Time:

Card:
27

Tarot Deck:

Moon Phase:

The Question I Am Asking Today:

The Card Drawn:

Related element:

◯ Fire ◯ Earth
◯ Water ◯ Air

Notes or interpretation for this card:

Describe in words or draw the card

In answer to my question, what message or guidance can I take from this card?

Keywords for this card:

I have entered this card on the:

◯ List of Cards Drawn in Order (pg 132)

◯ List of Cards Drawn by Date (pg 136, etc)

Date:

Time:

Card:
28

Tarot Deck:

Moon Phase:

The Question I Am Asking Today:

The Card Drawn:

Related element:

- Fire
- Earth
- Water
- Air

Notes or interpretation for this card:

Describe in words or draw the card

In answer to my question, what message or guidance can I take from this card?

Keywords for this card:

I have entered this card on the:

- List of Cards Drawn in Order (pg 132)
- List of Cards Drawn by Date (pg 136, etc)

Date:

Time:

Card:
29

Tarot Deck:

Moon Phase:

The Question I Am Asking Today:

The Card Drawn:

Related element:
◯ Fire ◯ Earth
◯ Water ◯ Air

Notes or interpretation for this card:

Describe in words or draw the card

In answer to my question, what message or guidance can I take from this card?

Keywords for this card:

I have entered this card on the:

◯ List of Cards Drawn in Order (pg 132)

◯ List of Cards Drawn by Date (pg 136, etc)

Date:

Time:

Card: 30

Tarot Deck:

Moon Phase:

The Question I Am Asking Today:

The Card Drawn:

Related element:

- Fire
- Earth
- Water
- Air

Notes or interpretation for this card:

Describe in words or draw the card

In answer to my question, what message or guidance can I take from this card?

Keywords for this card:

I have entered this card on the:

- List of Cards Drawn in Order (pg 132)
- List of Cards Drawn by Date (pg 136, etc)

Reflection Questions for Cards 1 to 30

How comfortable am I now with tarot cards since completing 30 card draws?

What have I noticed or learned from drawing 30 single cards?

Has anything changed in me since I began this process?

Have there been any trends in the types of cards I have pulled? (Refer to page 132)

Am I still working on my own or with the same teachers? Have I consulted anyone new?

My thoughts at this point in my tarot journey:

My Card Draws

for

Cards 31 to 60

Date:

Time:

Card:
31

Tarot Deck:

Moon Phase:

The Question I Am Asking Today:

The Card Drawn:

Related element:
- Fire
- Earth
- Water
- Air

Notes or interpretation for this card:

Describe in words or draw the card

In answer to my question, what message or guidance can I take from this card?

Keywords for this card:

I have entered this card on the:
- List of Cards Drawn in Order (pg 132)
- List of Cards Drawn by Date (pg 136, etc)

Date:

Time:

Card: 32

Tarot Deck:

Moon Phase:

The Question I Am Asking Today:

The Card Drawn:

Related element:

- Fire
- Earth
- Water
- Air

Notes or interpretation for this card:

Describe in words or draw the card

In answer to my question, what message or guidance can I take from this card?

Keywords for this card:

I have entered this card on the:

- List of Cards Drawn in Order (pg 132)
- List of Cards Drawn by Date (pg 136, etc)

Date:

Time:

Card: 33

Tarot Deck:

Moon Phase:

The Question I Am Asking Today:

The Card Drawn:

Related element:

◯ Fire ◯ Earth
◯ Water ◯ Air

Notes or interpretation for this card:

Describe in words or draw the card

In answer to my question, what message or guidance can I take from this card?

Keywords for this card:

I have entered this card on the:

◯ List of Cards Drawn in Order (pg 132)

◯ List of Cards Drawn by Date (pg 136, etc)

Date:

Time:

Card:
34

Tarot Deck:

Moon Phase:

The Question I Am Asking Today:

The Card Drawn:

Related element:
- Fire
- Earth
- Water
- Air

Notes or interpretation for this card:

Describe in words or draw the card

In answer to my question, what message or guidance can I take from this card?

Keywords for this card:

I have entered this card on the:
- List of Cards Drawn in Order (pg 132)
- List of Cards Drawn by Date (pg 136, etc)

DATE:

TIME:

CARD:
35

TAROT DECK:

MOON PHASE:

THE QUESTION I AM ASKING TODAY:

THE CARD DRAWN:

RELATED ELEMENT:
- FIRE
- EARTH
- WATER
- AIR

NOTES OR INTERPRETATION FOR THIS CARD:

DESCRIBE IN WORDS OR DRAW THE CARD

IN ANSWER TO MY QUESTION, WHAT MESSAGE OR GUIDANCE CAN I TAKE FROM THIS CARD?

KEYWORDS FOR THIS CARD:

I HAVE ENTERED THIS CARD ON THE:
- List of Cards Drawn in Order (pg 132)
- List of Cards Drawn by Date (pg 136, etc)

Date:

Time:

Card:
36

Tarot Deck:

Moon Phase:

The Question I Am Asking Today:

The Card Drawn:

Related element:

- ◯ Fire
- ◯ Earth
- ◯ Water
- ◯ Air

Notes or interpretation for this card:

Describe in words or draw the card

In answer to my question, what message or guidance can I take from this card?

Keywords for this card:

I have entered this card on the:

- ◯ List of Cards Drawn in Order (pg 132)
- ◯ List of Cards Drawn by Date (pg 136, etc)

Date:

Time:

Card: 37

Tarot Deck:

Moon Phase:

The Question I Am Asking Today:

The Card Drawn:

Related element:

- Fire
- Earth
- Water
- Air

Notes or interpretation for this card:

Describe in words or draw the card

In answer to my question, what message or guidance can I take from this card?

Keywords for this card:

I have entered this card on the:

- List of Cards Drawn in Order (pg 132)
- List of Cards Drawn by Date (pg 136, etc)

Date:

Time:

Card:
38

Tarot Deck:

Moon Phase:

The Question I Am Asking Today:

The Card Drawn:

Related element:

- Fire
- Earth
- Water
- Air

Notes or interpretation for this card:

Describe in words or draw the card

In answer to my question, what message or guidance can I take from this card?

Keywords for this card:

I have entered this card on the:

- List of Cards Drawn in Order (pg 132)
- List of Cards Drawn by Date (pg 136, etc)

Date:

Time:

Card: 39

Tarot Deck:

Moon Phase:

The Question I Am Asking Today:

The Card Drawn:

Related element:

- Fire
- Earth
- Water
- Air

Notes or interpretation for this card:

Describe in words or draw the card

In answer to my question, what message or guidance can I take from this card?

Keywords for this card:

I have entered this card on the:

- List of Cards Drawn in Order (pg 132)
- List of Cards Drawn by Date (pg 136, etc)

Date:

Time:

Card:
40

Tarot Deck:

Moon Phase:

The Question I Am Asking Today:

The Card Drawn:

Related element:

- Fire
- Earth
- Water
- Air

Notes or interpretation for this card:

Describe in words or draw the card

In answer to my question, what message or guidance can I take from this card?

Keywords for this card:

I have entered this card on the:

- List of Cards Drawn in Order (pg 132)
- List of Cards Drawn by Date (pg 136, etc)

Date:

Time:

Card:
41

Tarot Deck:

Moon Phase:

The Question I Am Asking Today:

The Card Drawn:

Related element:

- ◯ Fire
- ◯ Earth
- ◯ Water
- ◯ Air

Notes or interpretation for this card:

Describe in words or draw the card

In answer to my question, what message or guidance can I take from this card?

Keywords for this card:

I have entered this card on the:

- ◯ List of Cards Drawn in Order (pg 132)
- ◯ List of Cards Drawn by Date (pg 136, etc)

Date:

Time:

Card: 42

Tarot Deck:

Moon Phase:

The Question I Am Asking Today:

The Card Drawn:

Related element:
- ◯ Fire
- ◯ Earth
- ◯ Water
- ◯ Air

Notes or interpretation for this card:

Describe in words or draw the card

In answer to my question, what message or guidance can I take from this card?

Keywords for this card:

I have entered this card on the:
- ◯ List of Cards Drawn in Order (pg 132)
- ◯ List of Cards Drawn by Date (pg 136, etc)

Date:

Time:

Card:
43

Tarot Deck:

Moon Phase:

The Question I Am Asking Today:

The Card Drawn:

Related element:
- ◯ Fire
- ◯ Earth
- ◯ Water
- ◯ Air

Notes or interpretation for this card:

Describe in words or draw the card

In answer to my question, what message or guidance can I take from this card?

Keywords for this card:

I have entered this card on the:
- ◯ List of Cards Drawn in Order (pg 132)
- ◯ List of Cards Drawn by Date (pg 136, etc)

Date:

Time:

Card:
44

Tarot Deck:

Moon Phase:

The Question I Am Asking Today:

The Card Drawn:

Related element:
- Fire
- Earth
- Water
- Air

Notes or interpretation for this card:

Describe in words or draw the card

In answer to my question, what message or guidance can I take from this card?

Keywords for this card:

I have entered this card on the:
- List of Cards Drawn in Order (pg 132)
- List of Cards Drawn by Date (pg 136, etc)

Date:

Time:

Card:
45

Tarot Deck:

Moon Phase:

The Question I Am Asking Today:

The Card Drawn:

Related element:

- Fire
- Earth
- Water
- Air

Notes or interpretation for this card:

Describe in words or draw the card

In answer to my question, what message or guidance can I take from this card?

Keywords for this card:

I have entered this card on the:

- List of Cards Drawn in Order (pg 132)
- List of Cards Drawn by Date (pg 136, etc)

Date:

Time:

Card: 46

Tarot Deck:

Moon Phase:

The Question I Am Asking Today:

The Card Drawn:

Related element:

- Fire
- Earth
- Water
- Air

Notes or interpretation for this card:

Describe in words or draw the card

In answer to my question, what message or guidance can I take from this card?

Keywords for this card:

I have entered this card on the:

- List of Cards Drawn in Order (pg 132)
- List of Cards Drawn by Date (pg 136, etc)

Date:

Time:

Card:
47

Tarot Deck:

Moon Phase:

The Question I Am Asking Today:

Related element:

◯ Fire ◯ Earth
◯ Water ◯ Air

The Card Drawn:

Notes or interpretation for this card:

Describe in words or draw the card

In answer to my question, what message or guidance can I take from this card?

Keywords for this card:

I have entered this card on the:

◯ List of Cards Drawn in Order (pg 132)

◯ List of Cards Drawn by Date (pg 136, etc)

Date:

Time:

Card:
48

Tarot Deck:

Moon Phase:

The Question I Am Asking Today:

The Card Drawn:

Related element:
- Fire
- Earth
- Water
- Air

Notes or interpretation for this card:

Describe in words or draw the card

In answer to my question, what message or guidance can I take from this card?

Keywords for this card:

I have entered this card on the:
- List of Cards Drawn in Order (pg 132)
- List of Cards Drawn by Date (pg 136, etc)

Date:

Time:

Card:
49

Tarot Deck:

Moon Phase:

The Question I Am Asking Today:

The Card Drawn:

Related element:
- ◯ Fire
- ◯ Earth
- ◯ Water
- ◯ Air

Notes or interpretation for this card:

Describe in words or draw the card

In answer to my question, what message or guidance can I take from this card?

Keywords for this card:

I have entered this card on the:
- ◯ List of Cards Drawn in Order (pg 132)
- ◯ List of Cards Drawn by Date (pg 136, etc)

Date:

Time:

Card: 50

Tarot Deck:

Moon Phase:

The Question I Am Asking Today:

The Card Drawn:

Related element:

- Fire
- Earth
- Water
- Air

Notes or interpretation for this card:

Describe in words or draw the card

In answer to my question, what message or guidance can I take from this card?

Keywords for this card:

I have entered this card on the:

- List of Cards Drawn in Order (pg 132)
- List of Cards Drawn by Date (pg 136, etc)

Date:

Time:

Card:
51

Tarot Deck:

Moon Phase:

The Question I Am Asking Today:

The Card Drawn:

Related element:

◯ Fire ◯ Earth
◯ Water ◯ Air

Notes or interpretation for this card:

Describe in words or draw the card

In answer to my question, what message or guidance can I take from this card?

Keywords for this card:

I have entered this card on the:

◯ List of Cards Drawn in Order (pg 132)

◯ List of Cards Drawn by Date (pg 136, etc)

Date:

Time:

Card:
52

Tarot Deck:

Moon Phase:

The Question I Am Asking Today:

The Card Drawn:

Related element:

- Fire
- Earth
- Water
- Air

Notes or interpretation for this card:

Describe in words or draw the card

In answer to my question, what message or guidance can I take from this card?

Keywords for this card:

I have entered this card on the:

- List of Cards Drawn in Order (pg 132)
- List of Cards Drawn by Date (pg 136, etc)

Date:

Time:

Card:
53

Tarot Deck:

Moon Phase:

The Question I Am Asking Today:

The Card Drawn:

Related element:
- Fire
- Earth
- Water
- Air

Notes or interpretation for this card:

Describe in words or draw the card

In answer to my question, what message or guidance can I take from this card?

Keywords for this card:

I have entered this card on the:
- List of Cards Drawn in Order (pg 132)
- List of Cards Drawn by Date (pg 136, etc)

Date:

Time:

Card:
54

Tarot Deck:

Moon Phase:

The Question I Am Asking Today:

The Card Drawn:

Related element:

◯ Fire ◯ Earth
◯ Water ◯ Air

Notes or interpretation for this card:

Describe in words or draw the card

In answer to my question, what message or guidance can I take from this card?

Keywords for this card:

I have entered this card on the:

◯ List of Cards Drawn in Order (pg 132)

◯ List of Cards Drawn by Date (pg 136, etc)

Date:

Time:

Card:
55

Tarot Deck:

Moon Phase:

The Question I Am Asking Today:

The Card Drawn:

Related element:

◯ Fire ◯ Earth
◯ Water ◯ Air

Notes or interpretation for this card:

Describe in words or draw the card

In answer to my question, what message or guidance can I take from this card?

Keywords for this card:

I have entered this card on the:

◯ List of Cards Drawn in Order (pg 132)

◯ List of Cards Drawn by Date (pg 136, etc)

Date:

Time:

Card: 56

Tarot Deck:

Moon Phase:

The Question I Am Asking Today:

The Card Drawn:

Related element:

- ◯ Fire
- ◯ Earth
- ◯ Water
- ◯ Air

Notes or interpretation for this card:

Describe in words or draw the card

In answer to my question, what message or guidance can I take from this card?

Keywords for this card:

I have entered this card on the:

- ◯ List of Cards Drawn in Order (pg 132)
- ◯ List of Cards Drawn by Date (pg 136, etc)

Date:

Time:

Card:
57

Tarot Deck:

Moon Phase:

The Question I Am Asking Today:

The Card Drawn:

Related element:
- Fire
- Earth
- Water
- Air

Notes or interpretation for this card:

Describe in words or draw the card

In answer to my question, what message or guidance can I take from this card?

Keywords for this card:

I have entered this card on the:
- List of Cards Drawn in Order (pg 132)
- List of Cards Drawn by Date (pg 136, etc)

Date:

Time:

Card: 58

Tarot Deck:

Moon Phase:

The Question I Am Asking Today:

The Card Drawn:

Related element:

- Fire
- Earth
- Water
- Air

Notes or interpretation for this card:

Describe in words or draw the card

In answer to my question, what message or guidance can I take from this card?

Keywords for this card:

I have entered this card on the:

- List of Cards Drawn in Order (pg 132)
- List of Cards Drawn by Date (pg 136, etc)

Date:

Time:

Card:
59

Tarot Deck:

Moon Phase:

The Question I Am Asking Today:

The Card Drawn:

Related element:
- ◯ Fire
- ◯ Earth
- ◯ Water
- ◯ Air

Notes or interpretation for this card:

Describe in words or draw the card

In answer to my question, what message or guidance can I take from this card?

Keywords for this card:

I have entered this card on the:
- ◯ List of Cards Drawn in Order (pg 132)
- ◯ List of Cards Drawn by Date (pg 136, etc)

Date:

Time:

Card:
60

Tarot Deck:

Moon Phase:

The Question I Am Asking Today:

The Card Drawn:

Related element:

◯ Fire ◯ Earth
◯ Water ◯ Air

Notes or interpretation for this card:

Describe in words or draw the card

In answer to my question, what message or guidance can I take from this card?

Keywords for this card:

I have entered this card on the:

◯ List of Cards Drawn in Order (pg 132)

◯ List of Cards Drawn by Date (pg 136, etc)

Reflection Questions for Cards 31 to 60

How comfortable am I now with tarot cards since completing 60 single card draws?

What have I noticed or learned from drawing 60 single cards?

Has anything changed in me since I began this process?

Have there been any trends in the types of cards I have pulled? (Refer to page 133)

Am I still working on my own or with the same teachers? Have I consulted anyone new?

My thoughts at this point in my tarot journey:

My Card Draws

Cards 61 to 90

Date:

Time:

Card: 61

Tarot Deck:

Moon Phase:

The Question I Am Asking Today:

The Card Drawn:

Related element:

- Fire
- Earth
- Water
- Air

Notes or interpretation for this card:

Describe in words or draw the card

In answer to my question, what message or guidance can I take from this card?

Keywords for this card:

I have entered this card on the:

- List of Cards Drawn in Order (pg 132)
- List of Cards Drawn by Date (pg 136, etc)

Date:

Time:

Card:
62

Tarot Deck:

Moon Phase:

The Question I Am Asking Today:

The Card Drawn:

Related element:
- Fire
- Earth
- Water
- Air

Notes or interpretation for this card:

Describe in words or draw the card

In answer to my question, what message or guidance can I take from this card?

Keywords for this card:

I have entered this card on the:
- List of Cards Drawn in Order (pg 132)
- List of Cards Drawn by Date (pg 136, etc)

Date:

Time:

Card:
63

Tarot Deck:

Moon Phase:

The Question I Am Asking Today:

The Card Drawn:

Related element:
- Fire
- Earth
- Water
- Air

Notes or interpretation for this card:

Describe in words or draw the card

In answer to my question, what message or guidance can I take from this card?

Keywords for this card:

I have entered this card on the:
- List of Cards Drawn in Order (pg 132)
- List of Cards Drawn by Date (pg 136, etc)

Date:

Time:

Card:
64

Tarot Deck:

Moon Phase:

The Question I Am Asking Today:

The Card Drawn:

Related element:

- ◯ Fire
- ◯ Earth
- ◯ Water
- ◯ Air

Notes or interpretation for this card:

Describe in words or draw the card

In answer to my question, what message or guidance can I take from this card?

Keywords for this card:

I have entered this card on the:

- ◯ List of Cards Drawn in Order (pg 132)
- ◯ List of Cards Drawn by Date (pg 136, etc)

Date:

Time:

Card:
65

Tarot Deck:

Moon Phase:

The Question I Am Asking Today:

The Card Drawn:

Related element:

◯ Fire ◯ Earth
◯ Water ◯ Air

Notes or interpretation for this card:

Describe in words or draw the card

In answer to my question, what message or guidance can I take from this card?

Keywords for this card:

I have entered this card on the:

◯ List of Cards Drawn in Order (pg 132)

◯ List of Cards Drawn by Date (pg 136, etc)

Date:

Time:

Card: 66

Tarot Deck:

Moon Phase:

The Question I Am Asking Today:

The Card Drawn:

Related element:

- Fire
- Earth
- Water
- Air

Notes or interpretation for this card:

Describe in words or draw the card

In answer to my question, what message or guidance can I take from this card?

Keywords for this card:

I have entered this card on the:

- List of Cards Drawn in Order (pg 132)
- List of Cards Drawn by Date (pg 136, etc)

Date:

Time:

Card: 67

Tarot Deck:

Moon Phase:

The Question I Am Asking Today:

The Card Drawn:

Related element:

- Fire
- Earth
- Water
- Air

Notes or interpretation for this card:

Describe in words or draw the card

In answer to my question, what message or guidance can I take from this card?

Keywords for this card:

I have entered this card on the:

- List of Cards Drawn in Order (pg 132)
- List of Cards Drawn by Date (pg 136, etc)

Date:

Time:

Card: 68

Tarot Deck:

Moon Phase:

The Question I Am Asking Today:

The Card Drawn:

Related element:

- Fire
- Earth
- Water
- Air

Notes or interpretation for this card:

Describe in words or draw the card

In answer to my question, what message or guidance can I take from this card?

Keywords for this card:

I have entered this card on the:

- List of Cards Drawn in Order (pg 132)
- List of Cards Drawn by Date (pg 136, etc)

Date:

Time:

Card:
69

Tarot Deck:

Moon Phase:

The Question I Am Asking Today:

The Card Drawn:

Related element:

- ◯ Fire
- ◯ Earth
- ◯ Water
- ◯ Air

Notes or interpretation for this card:

Describe in words or draw the card

In answer to my question, what message or guidance can I take from this card?

Keywords for this card:

I have entered this card on the:

- ◯ List of Cards Drawn in Order (pg 132)
- ◯ List of Cards Drawn by Date (pg 136, etc)

DATE:

TIME:

CARD:
70

TAROT DECK:

MOON PHASE:

THE QUESTION I AM ASKING TODAY:

THE CARD DRAWN:

RELATED ELEMENT:
- ◯ FIRE
- ◯ EARTH
- ◯ WATER
- ◯ AIR

NOTES OR INTERPRETATION FOR THIS CARD:

DESCRIBE IN WORDS OR DRAW THE CARD

IN ANSWER TO MY QUESTION, WHAT MESSAGE OR GUIDANCE CAN I TAKE FROM THIS CARD?

KEYWORDS FOR THIS CARD:

I HAVE ENTERED THIS CARD ON THE:
- ◯ List of Cards Drawn in Order (pg 132)
- ◯ List of Cards Drawn by Date (pg 136, etc)

Date:

Time:

Card:
71

Tarot Deck:

Moon Phase:

The Question I Am Asking Today:

The Card Drawn:

Related element:

- Fire
- Earth
- Water
- Air

Notes or interpretation for this card:

Describe in words or draw the card

In answer to my question, what message or guidance can I take from this card?

Keywords for this card:

I have entered this card on the:

- List of Cards Drawn in Order (pg 132)
- List of Cards Drawn by Date (pg 136, etc)

Date:

Time:

Card:
72

Tarot Deck:

Moon Phase:

The Question I Am Asking Today:

The Card Drawn:

Related element:

◯ Fire ◯ Earth
◯ Water ◯ Air

Notes or interpretation for this card:

Describe in words or draw the card

In answer to my question, what message or guidance can I take from this card?

Keywords for this card:

I have entered this card on the:

◯ List of Cards Drawn in Order (pg 132)

◯ List of Cards Drawn by Date (pg 136, etc)

Date:

Time:

Card:
73

Tarot Deck:

Moon Phase:

The Question I Am Asking Today:

The Card Drawn:

Related element:
- ◯ Fire
- ◯ Earth
- ◯ Water
- ◯ Air

Notes or interpretation for this card:

Describe in words or draw the card

In answer to my question, what message or guidance can I take from this card?

Keywords for this card:

I have entered this card on the:
- ◯ List of Cards Drawn in Order (pg 132)
- ◯ List of Cards Drawn by Date (pg 136, etc)

Date:

Time:

Card: 74

Tarot Deck:

Moon Phase:

The Question I Am Asking Today:

The Card Drawn:

Related element:

- Fire
- Earth
- Water
- Air

Notes or interpretation for this card:

Describe in words or draw the card

In answer to my question, what message or guidance can I take from this card?

Keywords for this card:

I have entered this card on the:

- List of Cards Drawn in Order (pg 132)
- List of Cards Drawn by Date (pg 136, etc)

Date:

Time:

Card: 75

Tarot Deck:

Moon Phase:

The Question I Am Asking Today:

The Card Drawn:

Related element:

- Fire
- Earth
- Water
- Air

Notes or interpretation for this card:

Describe in words or draw the card

In answer to my question, what message or guidance can I take from this card?

Keywords for this card:

I have entered this card on the:

- List of Cards Drawn in Order (pg 132)
- List of Cards Drawn by Date (pg 136, etc)

Date:

Time:

Card:
76

Tarot Deck:

Moon Phase:

The Question I Am Asking Today:

The Card Drawn:

Related element:

- Fire
- Earth
- Water
- Air

Notes or interpretation for this card:

Describe in words or draw the card

In answer to my question, what message or guidance can I take from this card?

Keywords for this card:

I have entered this card on the:

- List of Cards Drawn in Order (pg 132)
- List of Cards Drawn by Date (pg 136, etc)

Date:

Time:

Card:
77

Tarot Deck:

Moon Phase:

The Question I Am Asking Today:

The Card Drawn:

Related element:

Fire
Earth
Water
Air

Notes or interpretation for this card:

Describe in words or draw the card

In answer to my question, what message or guidance can I take from this card?

Keywords for this card:

I have entered this card on the:

- List of Cards Drawn in Order (pg 132)
- List of Cards Drawn by Date (pg 136, etc)

Date:

Time:

Card:
78

Tarot Deck:

Moon Phase:

The Question I Am Asking Today:

The Card Drawn:

Related element:
- ◯ Fire
- ◯ Earth
- ◯ Water
- ◯ Air

Notes or interpretation for this card:

Describe in words or draw the card

In answer to my question, what message or guidance can I take from this card?

Keywords for this card:

I have entered this card on the:
- ◯ List of Cards Drawn in Order (pg 132)
- ◯ List of Cards Drawn by Date (pg 136, etc)

Date:

Time:

Card: 79

Tarot Deck:

Moon Phase:

The Question I Am Asking Today:

The Card Drawn:

Related element:

- ○ Fire
- ○ Earth
- ○ Water
- ○ Air

Notes or interpretation for this card:

Describe in words or draw the card

In answer to my question, what message or guidance can I take from this card?

Keywords for this card:

I have entered this card on the:

- ○ List of Cards Drawn in Order (pg 132)
- ○ List of Cards Drawn by Date (pg 136, etc)

Date:

Time:

Card: 80

Tarot Deck:

Moon Phase:

The Question I Am Asking Today:

The Card Drawn:

Related element:

- ◯ Fire
- ◯ Earth
- ◯ Water
- ◯ Air

Notes or interpretation for this card:

Describe in words or draw the card

In answer to my question, what message or guidance can I take from this card?

Keywords for this card:

I have entered this card on the:

- ◯ List of Cards Drawn in Order (pg 132)
- ◯ List of Cards Drawn by Date (pg 136, etc)

Date:

Time:

Card:
81

Tarot Deck:

Moon Phase:

The Question I Am Asking Today:

The Card Drawn:

Related element:

◯ Fire ◯ Earth
◯ Water ◯ Air

Notes or interpretation for this card:

Describe in words or draw the card

In answer to my question, what message or guidance can I take from this card?

Keywords for this card:

I have entered this card on the:

◯ List of Cards Drawn in Order (pg 132)

◯ List of Cards Drawn by Date (pg 136, etc)

Date:

Time:

Card:
82

Tarot Deck:

Moon Phase:

The Question I Am Asking Today:

The Card Drawn:

Related element:

- Fire
- Earth
- Water
- Air

Notes or interpretation for this card:

Describe in words or draw the card

In answer to my question, what message or guidance can I take from this card?

Keywords for this card:

I have entered this card on the:

- List of Cards Drawn in Order (pg 132)
- List of Cards Drawn by Date (pg 136, etc)

Date:

Time:

Card: 83

Tarot Deck:

Moon Phase:

The Question I Am Asking Today:

The Card Drawn:

Related element:

- Fire
- Earth
- Water
- Air

Notes or interpretation for this card:

Describe in words or draw the card

In answer to my question, what message or guidance can I take from this card?

Keywords for this card:

I have entered this card on the:

- List of Cards Drawn in Order (pg 132)
- List of Cards Drawn by Date (pg 136, etc)

Date:

Time:

Card: 84

Tarot Deck:

Moon Phase:

The Question I Am Asking Today:

The Card Drawn:

Related element:
- ◯ Fire
- ◯ Earth
- ◯ Water
- ◯ Air

Notes or interpretation for this card:

Describe in words or draw the card

In answer to my question, what message or guidance can I take from this card?

Keywords for this card:

I have entered this card on the:
- ◯ List of Cards Drawn in Order (pg 132)
- ◯ List of Cards Drawn by Date (pg 136, etc)

Date:

Time:

Card: 85

Tarot Deck:

Moon Phase:

The Question I Am Asking Today:

The Card Drawn:

Related element:

- Fire
- Earth
- Water
- Air

Notes or interpretation for this card:

Describe in words or draw the card

In answer to my question, what message or guidance can I take from this card?

Keywords for this card:

I have entered this card on the:

- List of Cards Drawn in Order (pg 132)
- List of Cards Drawn by Date (pg 136, etc)

Date:

Time:

Card:
86

Tarot Deck:

Moon Phase:

The Question I Am Asking Today:

The Card Drawn:

Related element:
- ◯ Fire
- ◯ Earth
- ◯ Water
- ◯ Air

Notes or interpretation for this card:

Describe in words or draw the card

In answer to my question, what message or guidance can I take from this card?

Keywords for this card:

I have entered this card on the:
- ◯ List of Cards Drawn in Order (pg 132)
- ◯ List of Cards Drawn by Date (pg 136, etc)

Date:

Time:

Card:
87

Tarot Deck:

Moon Phase:

The Question I Am Asking Today:

The Card Drawn:

Related element:

- Fire
- Earth
- Water
- Air

Notes or interpretation for this card:

Describe in words or draw the card

In answer to my question, what message or guidance can I take from this card?

Keywords for this card:

I have entered this card on the:

- List of Cards Drawn in Order (pg 132)
- List of Cards Drawn by Date (pg 136, etc)

Date:

Time:

Card:
88

Tarot Deck:

Moon Phase:

The Question I Am Asking Today:

The Card Drawn:

Related element:

◯ Fire ◯ Earth
◯ Water ◯ Air

Notes or interpretation for this card:

Describe in words or draw the card

In answer to my question, what message or guidance can I take from this card?

Keywords for this card:

I have entered this card on the:

◯ List of Cards Drawn in Order (pg 132)

◯ List of Cards Drawn by Date (pg 136, etc)

Date:

Time:

Card: 89

Tarot Deck:

Moon Phase:

The Question I Am Asking Today:

The Card Drawn:

Related element:

- Fire
- Earth
- Water
- Air

Notes or interpretation for this card:

Describe in words or draw the card

In answer to my question, what message or guidance can I take from this card?

Keywords for this card:

I have entered this card on the:

- List of Cards Drawn in Order (pg 132)
- List of Cards Drawn by Date (pg 136, etc)

Date:

Time:

Card: 90

Tarot Deck:

Moon Phase:

The Question I Am Asking Today:

The Card Drawn:

Related element:

◯ Fire ◯ Earth
◯ Water ◯ Air

Notes or interpretation for this card:

Describe in words or draw the card

In answer to my question, what message or guidance can I take from this card?

Keywords for this card:

I have entered this card on the:

◯ List of Cards Drawn in Order (pg 132)

◯ List of Cards Drawn by Date (pg 136, etc)

Reflection Questions for Cards 61 to 90

Were there any interesting things that happened in the last 30 draws?

Have there been any trends in the types of cards I have pulled in the final 30 cards?
(Refer to page 134)

Tarot Journey Reflection

- Completion Questions -

Tarot Journey Completion Questions

How comfortable am I now with tarot cards as compared to when I began this journey?

Did I achieve what I was hoping for from this study of the tarot?

If I was referring to any teachers, did I stay with the same one or ones, or seek out new teachers? Or, did I spend my time developing my own interpretations? Or, did I do both?

How intuitive do I feel now that I have completed 90 single card draws?

What have I noticed or learned from drawing 90 single cards?

Has anything changed in me since I began this process? (anything/nothing)

What card deck or decks did I use and what are my thoughts or feelings about them now?

Were some cards pulled more than once and some never pulled?

Were there any trends or themes in the cards that I pulled over the 90 cards? Suits? Elements? Repeats? Cards not drawn? What are my thoughts about these trends?

What are my thoughts now that I have completed this phase of my tarot journey and as I am going forward?

SECTION TWO

Resources & Tracking

LIST OF CARDS DRAWN IN ORDER

WITH TREND TRACKING

List of Cards Drawn in Order

With Trend Tracking

Cards 1 to 30:

	Element	Major Arcana	Minor Arcana				
Card 1		○	○	○	○	○	○
Card 2		○	○	○	○	○	○
Card 3		○	○	○	○	○	○
Card 4		○	○	○	○	○	○
Card 5		○	○	○	○	○	○
Card 6		○	○	○	○	○	○
Card 7		○	○	○	○	○	○
Card 8		○	○	○	○	○	○
Card 9		○	○	○	○	○	○
Card 10		○	○	○	○	○	○
Card 11		○	○	○	○	○	○
Card 12		○	○	○	○	○	○
Card 13		○	○	○	○	○	○
Card 14		○	○	○	○	○	○
Card 15		○	○	○	○	○	○
Card 16		○	○	○	○	○	○
Card 17		○	○	○	○	○	○
Card 18		○	○	○	○	○	○
Card 19		○	○	○	○	○	○
Card 20		○	○	○	○	○	○
Card 21		○	○	○	○	○	○
Card 22		○	○	○	○	○	○
Card 23		○	○	○	○	○	○
Card 24		○	○	○	○	○	○
Card 25		○	○	○	○	○	○
Card 26		○	○	○	○	○	○
Card 27		○	○	○	○	○	○
Card 28		○	○	○	○	○	○
Card 29		○	○	○	○	○	○
Card 30		○	○	○	○	○	○

Have there been any trends with the cards that have been drawn or no trend at all?

○ Yes? ○ No? Thoughts?

NOTE: Use this information in your reflection notes at the end of the the 1-30 card draw section.

List of Cards Drawn in Order

With Trend Tracking

Cards 31 to 60:

		Element	Major Arcana	Minor Arcana				
Card 31			○	○	○	○	○	○
Card 32			○	○	○	○	○	○
Card 33			○	○	○	○	○	○
Card 34			○	○	○	○	○	○
Card 35			○	○	○	○	○	○
Card 36			○	○	○	○	○	○
Card 37			○	○	○	○	○	○
Card 38			○	○	○	○	○	○
Card 39			○	○	○	○	○	○
Card 40			○	○	○	○	○	○
Card 41			○	○	○	○	○	○
Card 42			○	○	○	○	○	○
Card 43			○	○	○	○	○	○
Card 44			○	○	○	○	○	○
Card 45			○	○	○	○	○	○
Card 46			○	○	○	○	○	○
Card 47			○	○	○	○	○	○
Card 48			○	○	○	○	○	○
Card 49			○	○	○	○	○	○
Card 50			○	○	○	○	○	○
Card 51			○	○	○	○	○	○
Card 52			○	○	○	○	○	○
Card 53			○	○	○	○	○	○
Card 54			○	○	○	○	○	○
Card 55			○	○	○	○	○	○
Card 56			○	○	○	○	○	○
Card 57			○	○	○	○	○	○
Card 58			○	○	○	○	○	○
Card 59			○	○	○	○	○	○
Card 60			○	○	○	○	○	○

Have there been any trends with the cards that have been drawn or no trend at all?

○ Yes? ○ No? Thoughts? ______________________________

NOTE: Use this information in your reflection notes at the end of the the 31-60 card draw section.

List of Cards Drawn in Order
With Trend Tracking

Cards 61 to 90:

	Element	Major Arcana	Minor Arcana				
Card 61		○	○	○	○	○	○
Card 62		○	○	○	○	○	○
Card 63		○	○	○	○	○	○
Card 64		○	○	○	○	○	○
Card 65		○	○	○	○	○	○
Card 66		○	○	○	○	○	○
Card 67		○	○	○	○	○	○
Card 68		○	○	○	○	○	○
Card 69		○	○	○	○	○	○
Card 70		○	○	○	○	○	○
Card 71		○	○	○	○	○	○
Card 72		○	○	○	○	○	○
Card 73		○	○	○	○	○	○
Card 74		○	○	○	○	○	○
Card 75		○	○	○	○	○	○
Card 76		○	○	○	○	○	○
Card 77		○	○	○	○	○	○
Card 78		○	○	○	○	○	○
Card 79		○	○	○	○	○	○
Card 80		○	○	○	○	○	○
Card 81		○	○	○	○	○	○
Card 82		○	○	○	○	○	○
Card 83		○	○	○	○	○	○
Card 84		○	○	○	○	○	○
Card 85		○	○	○	○	○	○
Card 86		○	○	○	○	○	○
Card 87		○	○	○	○	○	○
Card 88		○	○	○	○	○	○
Card 89		○	○	○	○	○	○
Card 90		○	○	○	○	○	○

Have there been any trends with the cards that have been drawn or no trend at all?

○ Yes? ○ No? Thoughts? ______________________________

NOTE: Use this information in your reflection notes at the end of the the 61-90 card draw section.

LIST OF CARDS DRAWN BY DATE

List of Cards Drawn By Date

Major Arcana	Dates drawn
0 The Fool	
1 The Magician	
2 The High Priestess	
3 The Empress	
4 The Emperor	
5 The Hierophant	
6 The Lovers	
7 The Chariot	
8 Strength	
9 The Hermit	
10 Wheel of Fortune	
11 Justice	
12 The Hanged Man	
13 Death	
14 Temperance	
15 The Devil	
16 The Tower	
17 The Star	
18 The Moon	
19 The Sun	
20 Judgement	
21 The World	

Other Notes:

List of Cards Drawn By Date

Minor Arcana

Minor Arcana	Dates drawn
WANDS	
Ace of Wands	
Two of Wands	
Three of Wands	
Four of Wands	
Five of Wands	
Six of Wands	
Seven of Wands	
Eight of Wands	
Nine of Wands	
Ten of Wands	
Page of Wands	
Knight of Wands	
Queen of Wands	
King of Wands	
PENTACLES	
Ace of Pentacles	
Two of Pentacles	
Three of Pentacles	
Four of Pentacles	
Five of Pentacles	
Six of Pentacles	
Seven of Pentacles	
Eight of Pentacles	
Nine of Pentacles	
Ten of Pentacles	
Page of Pentacles	
Knight of Pentacles	
Queen of Pentacles	
King of Pentacles	

Other notes:

List of Cards Drawn By Date

Minor Arcana	Dates drawn
SWORDS	
Ace of Swords	
Two of Swords	
Three of Swords	
Four of Swords	
Five of Swords	
Six of Swords	
Seven of Swords	
Eight of Swords	
Nine of Swords	
Ten of Swords	
Page of Swords	
Knight of Swords	
Queen of Swords	
King of Swords	
CUPS	
Ace of Cups	
Two of Cups	
Three of Cups	
Four of Cups	
Five of Cups	
Six of Cups	
Seven of Cups	
Eight of Cups	
Nine of Cups	
Ten of Cups	
Page of Cups	
Knight of Cups	
Queen of Cups	
King of Cups	

Other notes:

MY NOTES FOR EACH CARD

My Notes For Each Card

Major Arcana
in general

My Notes For Each Card
Major Arcana

0 The Fool

1 The Magician

2 The High Priestess

3 The Empress

4 The Emperor

5 The Hierophant

6 The Lovers

7 The Chariot

My Notes For Each Card
Major Arcana

8 Strength

9 The Hermit

10 Wheel of Fortune

11 Justice

12 The Hanged Man

13 Death

14 Temperance

My Notes For Each Card
Major Arcana

15 The Devil

16 The Tower

17 The Star

18 The Moon

19 The Sun

20 Judgement

21 The World

My Notes For Each Card

Minor Arcana
in general

My Notes For Each Card

Minor Arcana - Wands

Wands in general

Ace of Wands

Two of Wands

Three of Wands

Four of Wands

Five of Wands

Six of Wands

Seven of Wands

Eight of Wands

Nine of Wands

Ten of Wands

Page of Wands

Knight of Wands

Queen of Wands

King of Wands

My Notes For Each Card

Minor Arcana - Pentacles

Pentacles in general

Ace of Pentacles

Two of Pentacles

Three of Pentacles

Four of Pentacles

Five of Pentacles

Six of Pentacles

Seven of Pentacles

Eight of Pentacles

Nine of Pentacles

Ten of Pentacles

Page of Pentacles

Knight of Pentacles

Queen of Pentacles

King of Pentacles

My Notes For Each Card

Minor Arcana - Swords

Swords in general

Ace of Swords

Two of Swords

Three of Swords

Four of Swords

Five of Swords

Six of Swords

Seven of Swords

Eight of Swords

Nine of Swords

Ten of Swords

Page of Swords

Knight of Swords

Queen of Swords

King of Swords

My Notes For Each Card

Minor Arcana - Cups

Cups in general

Ace of Cups

Two of Cups

Three of Cups

Four of Cups

Five of Cups

Six of Cups

Seven of Cups

Eight of Cups

Nine of Cups

Ten of Cups

Page of Cups

Knight of Cups

Queen of Cups

King of Cups

MY LIST OF QUESTIONS TO ASK

My List of Questions to Ask

SECTION THREE

Journal & Notes

BONUS SECTION

3-Card Spread

Date:

Time:

Tarot Deck:

Moon Phase:

The Question I Am Asking Today:

The Cards Drawn

(Describe in words or draw the cards)

Card #1 Represents:

Card #2 Represents:

Card #3 Represents:

Notes about this spread:

What message or guidance can I take from this spread?

DATE:

TIME:

TAROT DECK:

MOON PHASE:

THE QUESTION I AM ASKING TODAY:

THE CARDS DRAWN

(DESCRIBE IN WORDS OR DRAW THE CARDS)

CARD #1 REPRESENTS:

CARD #2 REPRESENTS:

CARD #3 REPRESENTS:

Notes about this spread:

What message or guidance can I take from this spread?

DATE:

TIME:

TAROT DECK:

MOON PHASE:

THE QUESTION I AM ASKING TODAY:

THE CARDS DRAWN

(DESCRIBE IN WORDS OR DRAW THE CARDS)

CARD #1 REPRESENTS:

CARD #2 REPRESENTS:

CARD #3 REPRESENTS:

Notes about this spread:

What message or guidance can I take from this spread?

DATE:

TIME:

TAROT DECK:

MOON PHASE:

THE QUESTION I AM ASKING TODAY:

THE CARDS DRAWN

(DESCRIBE IN WORDS OR DRAW THE CARDS)

CARD #1 REPRESENTS:

CARD #2 REPRESENTS:

CARD #3 REPRESENTS:

Notes about this spread:

What message or guidance can I take from this spread?

Date:

Time:

Tarot Deck:

Moon Phase:

The Question I Am Asking Today:

The Cards Drawn

(Describe in words or draw the cards)

Card #1 Represents:

Card #2 Represents:

Card #3 Represents:

Notes about this spread:

What message or guidance can I take from this spread?

Date:

Time:

Tarot Deck:

Moon Phase:

The Question I Am Asking Today:

The Cards Drawn

(Describe in words or draw the cards)

Card #1 Represents:

Card #2 Represents:

Card #3 Represents:

Notes about this spread:

What message or guidance can I take from this spread?

Dear Tarot Reader,

It is my sincere hope that this book has served you well on your journey in the realm of the Tarot!

Would you please do me a huge favour and leave a review on Amazon and share your experience of using this journal?

It would be greatly appreciated!

Cheers and thanks!
Soaring Raven

PS Please keep your eyes open for more of these types of books, including journals for multi-card Tarot spreads as well as our other journals and notebooks on Amazon and at aderynpublishing.com

Manufactured by Amazon.ca
Bolton, ON

23811280R00096